D1257789

ANIMALS ON THE BRINK

Japanese Macaques

Patricia Miller-Schroeder

www.av2books.com

AV² provides enriched content that supplements and complements this book. Weigl's AV² books strive to create inspired learning and engage young minds in a total learning experience.

Your AV² Media Enhanced books come alive with...

Audio
Listen to sections of the book read aloud.

Key Words
Study vocabulary, and complete a matching word activity.

Video
Watch informative video clips.

Quizzes
Test your knowledge.

Embedded Weblinks
Gain additional information for research.

Slide Show
View images and captions, and prepare a presentation.

Try This!
Complete activities and hands-on experiments.

... and much, much more!

Go to www.av2books.com, and enter this book's unique code.

BOOK CODE

R 2 4 0 3 9 2

AV² by Weigl brings you media enhanced books that support active learning.

Published by AV² by Weigl
350 5th Avenue, 59th Floor
New York, NY 10118
Website: www.av2books.com   www.weigl.com

Library of Congress Cataloging in Publication data available upon request.
Fax 1-866-449-3445 for the attention of the Publishing Records department

ISBN 978-1-62127-224-3 (hardcover)
ISBN 978-1-62127-225-0 (softcover)

Printed in the United States of America in North Mankato, Minnesota
1 2 3 4 5 6 7 8 9 17 16 15 14 13

032013
WEP300113

Project Coordinator Aaron Carr
Design Mandy Christiansen

Every reasonable effort has been made to trace ownership and to obtain permission to reprint copyright material. The publishers would be pleased to have any errors or omissions brought to their attention so that they may be corrected in subsequent printings.

Photo Credits
Weigl acknowledges Getty Images, Alamy, and iStockphoto as photo suppliers for this title.

Contents

Take a Stand

Debate · Research

The Japanese Macaque

A wonderfully unique type of monkey lives on the islands of Japan. The Japanese macaque lives farther north than any other nonhuman **primate**. Some groups of Japanese macaques live in areas that have a few months of very cold winter each year. These macaques are sometimes called "snow monkeys."

What is the Japanese macaque really like? In this book, you will visit the world of these fascinating creatures. You will discover how the monkeys communicate with one another using sounds and body movements. You will be amazed at the way many of them have learned to survive the cold winters of northern Japan. You will see how these monkeys live together in a troop and raise their young. So read on to enter the exciting world of the Japanese macaque.

Young macaques are covered in dark fur. As they grow older, their fur color changes. It can range from a light brown to several shades of gray.

Young monkeys learn the skills they need for survival at a very early age.

How to Take a Stand on an Issue

Research is important to the study of any scientific field. When scientists choose a subject to study, they must conduct research to ensure they have a thorough understanding of the topic. They ask questions about the subject and then search for answers. Sometimes, however, there is no clear answer to a question. In these cases, scientists must use the information they have to form a hypothesis, or theory. They must take a stand on one side of an issue or the other. Follow the process below for each Take a Stand section in this book to determine where you stand on these issues.

1. **What is the Issue?**
   a. Determine a research subject, and form a general question about the subject.

2. **Form a Hypothesis**
   a. Search at the library and online for sources of information on the subject.
   b. Conduct basic research on the subject to narrow down the general question.
   c. Form a hypothesis on the subject based on research to this point.
   d. Make predictions based on the hypothesis. What are the expected results?

3. **Research the Issue**
   a. Conduct extensive research using a variety of sources, including books, scientific journals, and reliable websites.
   b. Collect data on the issue and take notes on all information gathered from research.
   c. Draw conclusions based on the information collected.

4. **Conclusion**
   a. Explain the research findings.
   b. Was the hypothesis proved or disproved?

Monkey Business

Japanese macaques can live between 25 and 30 years. One hazard some macaques face is harsh winter weather. This can lead to food shortages. Other monkeys may die from injuries or illnesses. There are few natural predators where macaques live.

The largest Japanese macaques live in northern Japan's snow-covered mountains. This is the coldest part of the macaque's range.

Features

Japanese macaques are able to live in many types of **habitats** because they are **adaptable**. This is a feature they share with other monkeys and apes. Some macaques have special adaptations to cold weather, such as the thickness of their fur. Others have adaptations for life on a seaside beach, including the ability to dive and swim. Adaptations that make Japanese macaques very good at climbing trees enable many of them to live in mountain forests. Their flexibility has even allowed some of them to live in a hot, dry, desert environment. Like other primates, Japanese macaques are tough and clever, and they are able to learn quickly in new situations.

Japanese macaques are about the size of a cocker spaniel. When full grown, males are slightly larger than females. The weight of Japanese macaques varies from 20 to 40 pounds (9 to 18 kilograms). The average weight of males is 32 pounds (15 kg). For females, the average weight is 27 pounds (12 kg). Average height from head to rump is about 22.5 inches (57 centimeters) for males and 20.5 inches (52 cm) for females. Males can look even larger because they have more muscles and hair on their shoulders and hips.

Unlike many other types of monkeys, Japanese macaques have very short tails. On average, the length of the tail is a little over 3.5 inches (9 cm) in males. In females, the average length is slightly more than 3 inches (7.5 cm).

Japanese macaques are medium-sized, stocky monkeys. Their arms and legs are nearly equal in length, and they walk on all fours. Macaques are at home both in the trees and on the ground.

Macaques live on all of the Japanese islands except Hokkaido.

Classification

Japanese macaques belong to a large **order** of animals called primates. Primates include monkeys, apes, and prosimians, which are animals such as lemurs and lorises. Humans are also primates. Scientists do not agree on exactly how many **species** of primates there are today. The number is probably around 230 species. The smallest primate is the tiny mouse lemur, which weighs only 2 ounces (60 grams). The gorilla is the largest. Adult male gorillas can weigh as much as 400 pounds (180 kg). Japanese macaques are somewhere in the middle.

Japanese macaques belong to the group, or genus, of primates commonly called "Old World monkeys." This genus includes 22 species and can be found on the continents of Africa and Asia. The scientific, or Latin, name for the genus is *Macaca*. All Japanese macaques belong to the species *Macaca fuscata*, which includes two different types, or subspecies.

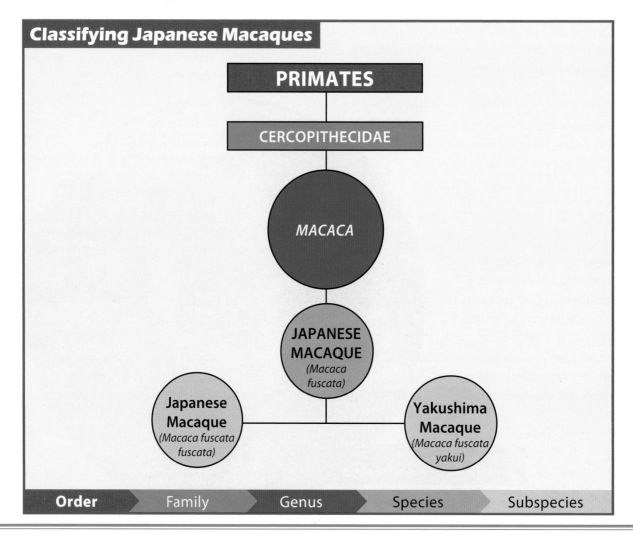

Classifying Japanese Macaques

PRIMATES

CERCOPITHECIDAE

MACACA

JAPANESE MACAQUE
(Macaca fuscata)

Japanese Macaque
(Macaca fuscata fuscata)

Yakushima Macaque
(Macaca fuscata yakui)

| Order | Family | Genus | Species | Subspecies |

The more common subspecies of Japanese macaques, *Macaca fuscata fuscata*, is found in most of Japan.

The subspecies *Macaca fuscata yakui* lives only on the small island of Yakushima in southern Japan.

The Barbary macaque, or *Macaca sylvanus*, is a close relative of the Japanese macaque. It is found mostly in the Atlas Mountains of North Africa.

Fur and Skin

Japanese macaque fur varies in color and length depending on where the animals live. The monkeys living in the coldest regions have long, gray-colored coats. Those in the warmer parts of their range have short, brown hair. In cold areas, a heavy winter coat is shed in the spring. When the cold weather returns in the fall, the heavy fur grows back. Male Japanese macaques often grow a longer cape of fur on their shoulders during the mating season.

Fur color can also vary with age. Young macaques usually have dark brown or black fur. The fur of older animals, even those living in warmer ranges, is often gray.

Japanese macaques are sometimes called red-faced macaques. They are called this because the pink skin on their faces and rumps changes to a deep red during the mating season. Old macaques sometimes have an uneven skin color that can appear faded.

Japanese macaques have special pads of hard skin on their rumps. These pads make it more comfortable for the animal to sit for long periods of time on hard surfaces. This feature is important because many macaques sleep sitting up in trees.

Eye color varies in Japanese macaques. Many of the monkeys have brown, orange, or yellowish eyes. Others have bright blue eyes.

Monkey Business

The name "snow monkey" is misleading since many Japanese macaques live in parts of southern Japan that have a warm climate year-round.

In the Shiga highlands on the Japanese island of Honshu, macaques live in a habitat where snow covers the ground for several months each year.

Special Adaptations

Japanese macaques have many special adaptations that help them live successfully in their different habitats.

Eyes

Sight is the most important sense to monkeys such as Japanese macaques. They have two large, forward-facing eyes. Macaques can judge distance and depth while moving and can sharply focus on movement around them. Like humans, macaques see in color. This lets them use color cues to find and identify food.

Teeth

An adult macaque has 32 teeth just like an adult human. Macaques have teeth for biting and slicing, as well as teeth for grinding and crushing. Male macaques have very large canine teeth.

Cheek Pouches

Macaques have large pouches inside their cheeks. These expand and can be packed full of food. This allows the monkeys to quickly gather a great deal of food.

Hands

Japanese macaque hands are much like human hands. Each hand has four flexible fingers and an **opposable** thumb. This lets Japanese macaques pinch their fingers and thumb together to grasp objects. Having hands that can grasp allows macaques to firmly hang on to branches. Macaques have tiny, raised ridges on their fingertips that help them feel and grip objects.

Feet

Like most primates, Japanese macaques have feet that are very similar to their hands. Their feet are flat with five toes. The big toes are opposable like the thumbs. This allows macaques to hold objects with their feet.

Groups

Japanese macaques live in social groups called troops. When they are young, the troop gives them a safe, secure place in which to grow. There is safety in numbers because the troop provides protection from predators. Food may be easier to find in a troop, since each troop has its own favorite feeding spots.

Female Japanese macaques spend their whole lives in their original troop. Most male Japanese macaques move from one troop to another when they mature. Many change troops several times. Some become wanderers, joining a troop only during the mating season.

There are almost always more adult females than adult males in a troop. Each troop also has several infants and **juvenile** members. Most troops have one top male and one top female. They are called the alpha male and the alpha female. The alpha male needs the alpha female's support to keep his position in the troop.

Both the alpha male and the alpha female settle disputes between troop members. All members have their special places based on whom they are related to or who their friends are. If disputes break out, monkeys depend on family or friends to support them.

The troop is organized around groups of closely related female monkeys. This type of group is called a matriline. A matriline may contain mothers, daughters, grandmothers, granddaughters, aunts, nieces, female cousins, and sisters.

Life in a troop tends to be very orderly. All members travel together when the troop changes its location.

Monkey Business

Troops of Japanese macaques usually contain 20 to 100 animals. If a troop becomes too large, it may break into two smaller troops.

In many troops, about half the monkeys are adults, and half are infants and children.

Monkey Business

Among Japanese macaques, young females are the most likely to pick up and pass on new ideas or behaviors. Adult males are the least likely to learn them.

Japanese macaques raised in captivity with other types of monkeys will continue to make the vocal sounds that macaques use. They do not start using the sounds of the other monkeys.

Communication

Japanese macaques are very intelligent animals. They have many different ways of communicating. Japanese macaques use different **vocalizations**, body language, and displays to send messages to one another.

Monkeys are usually noisy creatures, and Japanese macaques are no exception. Their vocabulary includes more than 30 types of sounds. These sounds include a variety of whistles, warbles, sq̶u̶e̶a̶l̶s̶, and ...

...cal communication is very important to ...e Japanese macaque. Vocalizations can ...used to find a mate, call other macaques ...lay, or warn others of danger.

...an Pavelka began studying the ...macaques of the Arashiyama ...in Dilley, Texas, in 1981. ...aches **primatology** at the ...f Calgary in Canada. Pavelka ...book, *Monkeys of the* ...ut her work with the ...exas snow monkeys.

"O... steppi... grass jus... in a near... walking ...

Mary Susan Pavelka

Body Language

Vocalizations are often combined with body language to send messages. Body language includes facial expressions or the way an animal moves its body. This means of communication lets other macaques know what mood a monkey is in, if it is ready for play, or if it just wants to be left alone.

Aggression

If one monkey stares at another, it is a threat. If the monkey wants to look even more threatening, it lowers its head, wrinkles its forehead, raises its eyebrows, and flattens its ears. It will then thrust out its mouth and make harsh, puffing sounds.

Displays

Japanese macaques have a special display that they use to announce their presence to other macaques. It is called the long-distance tree display. The full display involves swaying and shaking the tops of trees. A roaring vocalization is given at the same time. This display is usually given between males of neighboring troops. It can also be given by wandering males when they approach a strange troop during the mating season. High-ranking females may give the tree-shaking display, but they do not roar warnings.

Friendly

Monkeys who want to do something friendly, such as grooming, will smack their lips. Grooming is an important activity in a Japanese macaque troop. It brings troop members together in a pleasant social activity. Most grooming occurs between mothers and their offspring.

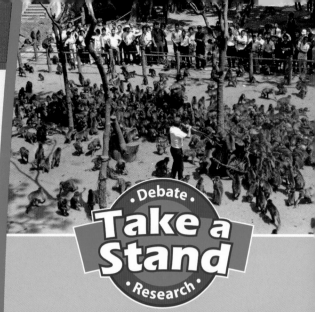

Play

Play is an important part of life in a macaque troop. Young Japanese macaques spend a great deal of time playing. Play allows them to test their strength and skills. It also teaches them about macaque social behavior. When animals want to play, they use a special "play face." In this signal, the mouth is wide open, and both top and bottom teeth show what looks like a grin.

Take a Stand
· Debate ·
· Research ·

Is it right to keep monkeys in zoos?

Zoos around the world house thousands of different animals, allowing people to view them in a safe and secure setting. Visitors to zoos hope to catch a glimpse of animals that they may never get to see in nature. Many of these zoos work hard to help save **threatened** and **endangered** species. However, some people argue that it is cruel to keep animals such as Japanese macaques in captivity away from their natural habitats.

FOR

1. By visiting zoos, the public gets to learn more about the Japanese macaque. This helps make people more aware of the difficulties macaques face in nature due to their shrinking habitat.
2. Zoos are ideal places to study the Japanese macaque. They provide scientists with a safe environment to conduct their research.

AGAINST

1. Japanese macaques are used to roaming large areas and should not be kept in a small, enclosed zoo environment.
2. Japanese macaques living in zoos can grow dependent on their human handlers and lose their abilities to survive in nature.

Monkey Business

A troop provides a safe, secure setting in which macaques can grow up. Most young are surrounded by relatives.

Japanese macaques are known to display strong family bonds. Scientists have found that even grandmothers take an active role in raising the young.

Mating and Birth

The mating season for Japanese macaques is fall and early winter. Mating at these times of year ensures that infants are not born in the cold winter months. Mating months vary depending on where the troop lives. In the southern part of Japan, the monkey mating season is from November to February. In the colder north, it lasts from October to December.

When the mating season occurs, the faces of Japanese macaques flush a bright red. This is because of **hormones** that are released in the animals' bodies at this time. Both females and males mate with many partners during a mating season. Young are born the following spring or early summer.

On average, a female gives birth every 1.5 to 3 years.

The **gestation period** for Japanese macaques is about six months. Most infants are born from mid-April to mid-July. When the mother is ready to give birth, she becomes restless and looks for a private spot. One of her female relatives may stay close by while she gives birth.

Japanese macaques are almost always born at night. It is safest to give birth while the troop is resting. That way, the mother will not be left behind while the troop moves during the day in search of food.

From an Expert

"A primate mother is much more than a warm body...and a milk supply. She is also the infant's introduction into the complex social world in which it must survive. Her behavior sets the stage upon which her offspring's social life drama will unfold."
- Linda M. Fedigan

Linda M. Fedigan began studying Japanese macaques in 1971 when the Arashiyama West troop was moved from Japan to Texas. She lived with the troop for more than three years. Fedigan teaches primatology at the University of Calgary. She has edited and written many books and articles on Japanese macaques and other primates.

Monkey Business

When a Japanese macaque is born, the mother is very protective. She will not let others come too close.

The bond formed between a mother macaque and her young may last a lifetime. A male that has left his troop may still recognize his mother if the two monkeys meet years later.

Infants

Newborn macaques are tiny and helpless. Soft baby fur covers their bodies. Big eyes stare out of tiny, wrinkled faces. Even though they look weak, infant macaques can cling to their mother's fur with their hands and feet. Shortly after birth, the infant begins feeding on its mother's milk. The mother cradles and supports her infant as it **nurses**.

The mother provides all of the care for the infant. Mother and baby must travel with the troop. The infant holds on to the fur on its mother's chest or belly as she walks on all fours. For the first few hours after birth, the mother walks on three legs and supports the infant with one hand. She grooms it during rest times and keeps it warm and safe.

By the time the baby macaque is a few months old, the mother will begin teaching the youngster what is good to eat and what is harmful. She encourages its attempts to walk and climb. She supervises its first attempts to play with other infants and comes to its aid whenever it calls for help.

Other members of the troop help care for the infant as it grows. Adult females and juvenile males and females groom it and keep it from wandering. Its older brothers and sisters pay special attention to it. An infant as young as three months can survive without its mother if another troop member adopts it. Males have been known to adopt older infants or **yearlings** that need attention. Males sometimes comfort, carry, protect, or play with young macaques. On the whole, the troop provides many caregivers who are willing to give young macaques attention and support.

Infant macaques depend almost entirely on their mother's milk for food during their first three months of life.

Development

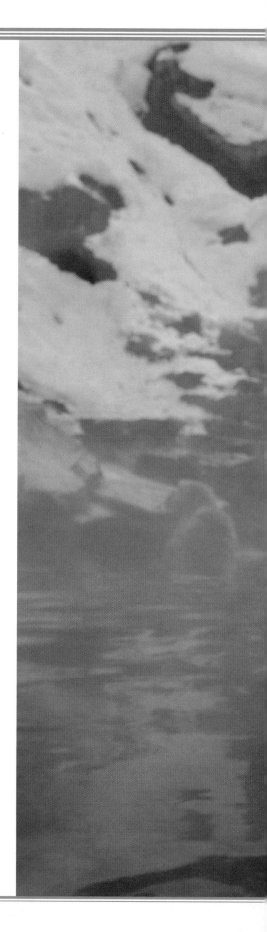

Newborn macaques weigh less than 1 pound (0.5 kg). Their tiny bodies measure only 4 inches (10 cm) long, and their fur is dark brown or black. Although they ride clinging to their mother at first, they can sit up and move around by 1 week of age. Nursing is their main source of food, but they begin tasting solid food as early as 2 weeks of age. Japanese macaques walk on all fours by 3 weeks. At this time, they begin to play with other infants.

The growing infant monkey sheds its dark baby coat by 3 months. The baby macaque now rides on its mother's back. At this time, young macaques begin looking for food with their mothers. They learn to stuff their cheek pouches. Most still nurse and come to their mothers for comfort and protection. By 4 months, baby macaques are chubby and furry, weighing about 4 pounds (2 kg).

Males and females begin to behave differently by 6 months. Females spend more time close to their mothers and other female relatives. Males spend more time with playmates in play groups away from their mothers. Both males and females forage, or search, for food on their own and eat everything adults do.

After the first year of life, young macaques are completely **weaned**. Males continue to spend more time away from their mothers. Their play is very active and noisy. Females show a growing interest in infants. They try playing mother. Both males and females like to swim and play in water.

Juvenile males spend most of their time in peer groups and associate with other males. Females become more involved with play-mothering and practice caring for infants. Females sometimes try new foods or behaviors that other troop members adopt.

Most female macaques will become mothers at about 5 years old. Males can mate at age 6 but will not be full size until they are 8 years old.

Females usually give birth to one infant at a time. Twins are rare.

Habitat

Japanese macaques live on most of the islands of Japan. They have adapted to a wide variety of climates. Much of their natural habitat lies in the mountain forests that once covered much of Japan. In the northern part of the macaques' range, snow blankets the ground from December to March. Snowdrifts are up to 13 feet (4 m) deep and cover most of the vegetation. Trees lose their leaves, and temperatures drop to 5° Fahrenheit (−15° Celsius). Some macaques live at elevations higher than 9,600 feet (2,900 m) above sea level.

Macaques that live through the cold winters of northern Japan keep warm by soaking in naturally occurring hot springs. There are many of these springs in the mountains. The water may be as warm as 109°F (43°C). The monkeys sit up to their necks in the steaming water. When they get out of the warm pools, they depend on their long coats of fur and quick movement to keep them warm. The macaques sometimes fluff out their fur, trapping air under the fur to help keep in body heat.

Organizing the Mountain Forest

Earth is home to millions of different **organisms**, all of which have specific survival needs. These organisms rely on their environment, or the place where they live, for their survival. All plants and animals have relationships with their environment. They interact with the environment itself, as well as the other plants and animals within the environment. These interactions create **ecosystems**.

Ecosystems can be broken down into levels of organization. These levels range from a single plant or animal to many species of plants and animals living together in an area.

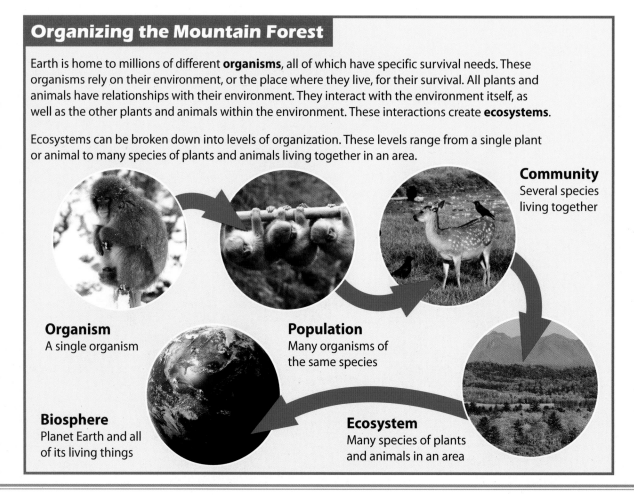

Organism
A single organism

Population
Many organisms of the same species

Community
Several species living together

Ecosystem
Many species of plants and animals in an area

Biosphere
Planet Earth and all of its living things

Monkey Business

At Jigokudani, or Hell's Valley, in northern Japan, macaques began using the mountain hot springs in 1963 when a young female went into a hot spring where soybeans had been scattered. Others soon followed her example.

Jigokudani, located near the town of Yamanouchi, is home to more than 200 Japanese macaques. It is not uncommon to find an entire troop using the area's hot springs to keep warm during the cold winter months.

The **home range** of Japanese macaques can vary in size depending on how much food there is to eat. Groups that live in the warmer south have no need for large home ranges. Food is plentiful year-round. Here, home ranges may be as small as 0.4 square miles (1 square kilometer). The average range in the south is 2 square miles (5 sq. km). In the north, where food is scarce for part of the year, home ranges may be 7 to 11 square miles (20 to 30 sq. km). Japanese macaques' home ranges are being upset in many areas by forest clearing. If this happens, the macaques must search an even larger area for food. They may have to cover 14 square miles (36 sq. km) or more. Troops' home ranges sometimes overlap. Most of the time, neighboring troops avoid each other. They let each other know where they are by shaking treetops. If they do meet, encounters are most often quiet, but fighting may occur.

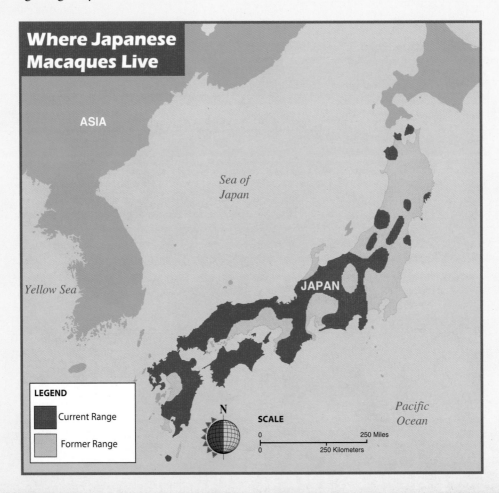

Where Japanese Macaques Live

ASIA

Sea of Japan

Yellow Sea

JAPAN

Pacific Ocean

LEGEND

Current Range

Former Range

N

SCALE

0   250 Miles

0   250 Kilometers

A troop travels to various parts of its home range depending on where the best food can be found at that time of year. Spring and fall are times of plenty. Food is available in many parts of the range.

In the winter months, northern macaques spend less time traveling. It takes a great deal of energy to move around through snowdrifts. During the cold season, snow monkeys will often sleep huddled together for warmth. They can form huge furry balls, with little faces peeking out of the fur. Groups of three or four monkeys have been seen lined up on tree branches, hugging each other front to back.

Some Japanese macaques live on the southern islands of Japan. Here, snow is not often seen, and most of the trees keep their leaves year-round.

·Debate· Take a Stand ·Research·

Should macaque troops be sent to other countries?

The Japanese macaque is quickly running out of living space. Its habitat is disappearing, and many macaques are being destroyed or trapped as crop-raiding pests. About 40 years ago, a "pest" macaque troop was successfully relocated to Texas. There, it has grown and thrived. It provides opportunities for scientists to study macaques in a new environment.

FOR

1. Setting up colonies of Japanese macaques in other countries gives more scientists and students in these countries a chance to study the primates without having to travel great distances.
2. Many of these pest troops would be destroyed if they were not relocated. Moving them saves the animals' lives.

AGAINST

1. Students of primate behavior can learn the most about Japanese macaques by studying them in their natural habitat.
2. Moving macaques does not solve the problem of their shrinking habitat.

Monkey Business

Most Japanese macaques are willing to try new foods. They learn the best way to handle unfamiliar food by trial and error and by watching other monkeys.

Japanese macaques sometimes eat the blossoms off cherry trees when these trees bloom in the early spring.

Diet

Japanese macaques are omnivores, which means they eat both plants and animals. Their natural habitats provide them with a wide variety of foods. Their favorite foods include fruits, berries, acorns, and nuts. However, they also eat leaves, grasses, seeds, flowers, green stalks, mushrooms, and fruit pits. In some areas, macaques eat algae and kelp that wash onto beaches.

The macaques' habitats also provide them with a variety of animal foods. They eat spiders, insects, larvae, snails, crabs, crayfish, and barnacles. Some take eggs from birds' nests.

The Japanese macaque's diet often varies by season. Fruits are a primary source of **nutrition** during the summer. In warmer habitats, fallen leaves, dug up roots, and herbs are important food sources in winter. Fungi such as mushrooms also provide food for hungry macaques.

Japanese macaques that live in colder northern regions have developed special feeding habits that help them survive. These snow monkeys live through a cold winter by using every bit of available food. They eat bark stripped from tree branches and twigs. They also search for and eat the trees' tightly curled winter buds and shoots.

Opposable thumbs allow macaques to pick up objects such as branches, fallen fruit, and even items as small as seeds. This makes feeding on a variety of food easier.

The Food Cycle

A food cycle shows how energy in the form of food is passed from one living thing to another. As Japanese macaques feed and move through their habitats, they affect the lives of the animals around them. The feeding habits of the macaques produce changes in the environment. In the diagram below, the arrows show the flow of energy from one living thing to another through a **food web**.

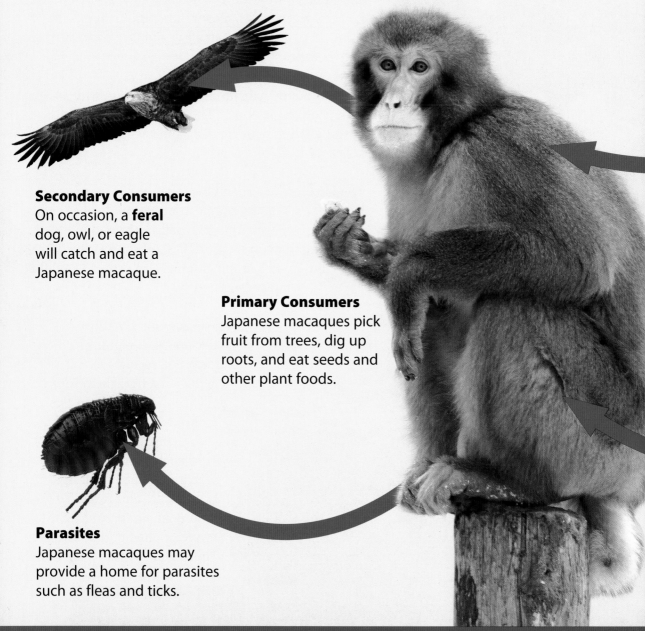

Secondary Consumers
On occasion, a **feral** dog, owl, or eagle will catch and eat a Japanese macaque.

Primary Consumers
Japanese macaques pick fruit from trees, dig up roots, and eat seeds and other plant foods.

Parasites
Japanese macaques may provide a home for parasites such as fleas and ticks.

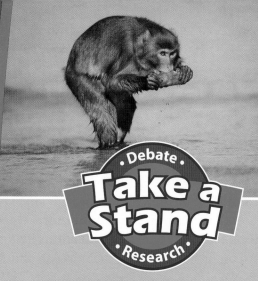

Producers
Plants grow from the soil and produce fruit.

Decomposers
When a Japanese macaque dies, decomposers found in the soil will break down the body, adding nutrients to the soil.

Omnivores
Although most of their diet consists of fruits and other plant foods, Japanese macaques, like many other monkey species, also eat fish, shellfish, insects, and eggs.

Take a Stand
Debate · Research

Should scientists provide food for troops of Japanese macaques found in nature?

Since the early 1950s, many Japanese researchers have set out food for the monkey troops they were studying. This was done to either bring the animals into an open area where they could be easily watched or to see how they reacted to new foods or situations. Sometimes, it was done to keep the monkeys from raiding farmers' fields.

FOR

1. Many discoveries about Japanese macaques have come from studies of monkeys provided with food. Scientists can continue to learn about macaque behavior by studying these troops.
2. By providing food, scientists keep hungry monkeys from starving or risking harm by going into farmers' fields to raid crops.

AGAINST

1. Providing troops with food changes the macaques' behavior. Scientists should learn about the monkeys by studying their natural behavior in their habitats.
2. Feeding causes troop sizes to become much larger, which may make it harder for a troop to find enough food from natural sources.

Competition

Most Japanese macaques do not usually have to compete with one another for food. When their natural habitats are not disturbed by humans, there is often enough for all. Troops avoid each other if possible. If troops meet, the encounters are often peaceful, and two troops may even travel together for a while. This is especially true for populations living on the larger islands of Japan, including Honshu, Shikoku, and Kyushu.

When living space and food are scarce, encounters between troops can turn violent. In one study of macaques on Yakushima Island, scientists observed a larger troop force out a smaller troop of macaques living in the same area. The scientists believed that the Yakushima subspecies is more likely to defend its territory, which may be a result of limited resources.

Males may compete for females in the mating season. Wandering males visit other troops at this time hoping for the chance to mate. However, females choose their mating partners. Sometimes, new males are welcomed. At other times, they are chased away.

The one serious natural enemy of Japanese macaques is humans. For centuries, people in Japan have hunted macaques for their fur and as a source of food. Today, humans are still the macaques' main competitors. As more and more of the macaques' habitats have been turned into farmland, some farmers try to destroy macaques as crop-raiding pests.

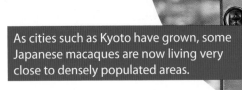

As cities such as Kyoto have grown, some Japanese macaques are now living very close to densely populated areas.

Male macaques' large canine teeth are often used for defense and during showdowns with other males.

Monkey Business

Very little interaction with predators has been seen among Japanese macaques. However, when a bobcat grabbed an infant from the macaque troop that was moved to Texas, it was chased and mobbed by the whole troop.

About 100,000 serows live in Japan. Most of their habitat overlaps the areas in which Japanese macaques live.

Japanese Macaques with Other Animals

Japanese macaques share their habitats with several other animals. As a result of habitat destruction, many of these creatures are disappearing. The Asiatic black bear still lives in Japan, but its numbers are not large. Bears, like macaques, are omnivores, but the two types of animals do not seem to compete. The serow, a type of goat-antelope, lives in Japan's mountain forests. In winter, the serow lives on twigs and branches, as the macaque does, but they do not compete either.

Other animals that macaques may encounter include the raccoon dog, red fox, pine marten, hare, badger, and flying squirrel. None of these animals interferes with the macaques. Eagles and large Ural owls may occasionally take a macaque infant. Packs of feral dogs sometimes hunt in the macaques' territories. However, Japanese macaques mostly live undisturbed by the other creatures in their habitats.

The Ural owl is active at night. It is common throughout Europe and northern Asia.

Folklore

The Japanese macaque has long been a part of Japanese folklore. In most tales, the monkeys have been considered very wise. The symbol of the Three Wise Monkeys who "See No Evil, Hear No Evil, and Speak No Evil" is based on the Japanese macaque.

Some people believe Japanese macaques bring good luck. Many visitors go to an ancient Buddhist monkey shrine at a place called Nara. Here, they touch an image of a smiling monkey in red robes, hoping it will bring them good luck.

Japan's monkeys have long been thought to protect children. Mothers sometimes give small monkey toys to children. Sometimes, they even sew small monkey figures on their children's clothing.

Monkeys are honored in Japan by having every 12th year named after them. Children who are born in the Year of the Monkey are believed to have the same traits the monkey has. These children are believed to be clever.

In old Japanese folktales, Japanese macaques are often shown as clever tricksters who outsmart other people. Sometimes, they even outsmart themselves. In tales such as "The Grateful Monkey's Secret" and "Monkey and the Crab," the story ends with the monkey learning a valuable lesson.

As part of the new-year celebrations when a Year of the Monkey begins, large wooden plaques with monkey faces are put up in Tokyo's busy shopping streets.

Myth	**VS**	Fact

Uttering a monkey's name can make good luck disappear. Touching a monkey statue can make good luck happen.

In Japan, some people think monkeys are symbols of good luck. The Japanese word for monkey, *saru*, also means "removing bad luck." However, there is no scientific evidence that Japanese macaques have anything to do with people's luck.

Monkeys are clever tricksters who will harm a human if given the chance.

Japanese macaques use their cleverness to find enough food and to keep their troop safe. They generally pose no threat to the safety of humans that are not trying to harm them.

Monkeys are dirty, messy animals. They smell bad and have no manners.

Japanese macaques spend a good deal of time grooming their fur to keep it clean. They smell no more than humans who do not wear deodorant. Monkeys have a very clear set of "monkey manners" that they follow to keep life in the troop running smoothly.

The Toshogu shrine, on the island of Honshu, includes a wood carving of the Three Wise Monkeys. Their names in Japanese are Mizaru, Kikazaru, and Iwazaru.

The Japanese macaques using the hot springs at Hell's Valley have grown used to all the attention they receive. Each year, thousands of tourists visit the site to see the monkeys and take pictures.

Status

Scientists do not know the true population of Japanese macaques living in nature. The estimates that are given do not provide a complete picture. It is thought that there could be up to 100,000 macaques living in troops across Japan, but it would be very difficult to prove that figure. In some areas, populations may be growing. In other areas, changes are occurring that affect the life and health of the macaque populations. These changes include loss of food sources, loss of habitat, and human interference. As a result, macaque populations in these areas are shrinking.

The Japanese macaque has been protected by the Japanese government since 1948. At that time, laws were passed banning its export, capture, or destruction. This does not mean the animals are safe. In areas where macaques raid crops, they may be classified as pests. The government can give permits for pest animals to be destroyed or captured. If this capture and destruction of macaques continues, many populations may disappear, and surviving populations may become increasingly unhealthy as they shrink in size.

From an Expert

"Many monkey populations are pests, partly because habitat destruction deprived them of natural foods. The pest populations may be the only monkey populations actually present in much of the country."
- David Sprague

David Sprague has been studying the Japanese macaques in nature on Yakushima Island for many years. He teaches at the University of Kyoto and coedits the "Japan Primate Newsletter." He is involved with saving Japanese macaques and their habitat.

Decline in Population

Loss of habitat is the biggest threat to the survival of Japanese macaques living in nature. The monkeys' habitat has been shrinking since the end of World War II in 1945. At that time, the Japanese government decided to develop the forest industry. Huge areas of natural forest were completely cut down, and the land was replanted with cedar trees. Lumber from cedars is used to build homes. These trees, however, do not provide food for macaques.

Natural forests have also been cut to make way for farmland, as well as for growing towns and cities. This reduces the available monkey habitat further. Even isolated areas are being developed into vacation sites such as ski resorts. Roads built to link resorts and cities cut through more monkey habitat. So much macaque habitat has been destroyed that some Japanese macaque populations have few places left to go. Hungry Japanese macaques searching for food raid crops and gardens. Sometimes, they spoil a whole harvest. They enter towns and cause damage.

Animals on the Brink

Farmers try to get rid of the monkeys by trapping or shooting them. Professional hunters capture hundreds of Japanese macaques each year. Some of the macaques that are trapped are moved to other areas. The fate of many others is not known.

The Japanese government now has a program to put up electric fences around farmland. This keeps the monkeys away from crops and reduces the chances that farmers will try to harm them. Still, the fences will not solve the problem of what the monkeys will eat or where they will go.

There is a limited amount of space on the Japanese islands for both macaques and people. At times, Japanese macaques are now spotted even in large urban areas, including Kyoto and Tokyo.

Take a Stand

Debate · *Research*

Should scientists use monkeys for medical and product research?

Monkeys are used by scientists for different types of research because they are very similar to people. Since monkeys and humans are both primates, many scientists believe that monkeys will often react to a drug, medical treatment, or product the same way that a human would.

FOR

1. Using monkeys for drug and product research can help save human lives by discovering new cures and safer products.
2. By studying the monkeys, scientists will also be able to better understand the different illnesses that threaten these animals.

AGAINST

1. Taking monkeys out of their natural habitat and placing them in laboratories for tests and research can be considered cruel and may be harmful to the monkeys.
2. Even though monkeys and humans are both primates, they also come from a different genus and species. Some drugs may affect the monkeys differently than they would a human.

Back from the Brink

Japanese macaque populations are declining all over Japan. For centuries, Japanese forests have provided everything the macaques needed to survive. Now, increasing pressure from Japan's growing population is causing the monkeys' forest home to shrink. This has forced the monkeys to live closer to populated areas where they are considered pests by the local residents.

In an effort to save the monkeys from being destroyed, Japanese scientists looked for long-term answers. One option was to find a new home for monkeys living in a reduced and endangered habitat. In 1972, an entire troop of close to 100 macaques was shipped to the United States. The troop was moved onto fenced ranch land in southern Texas. Although the monkeys were studied by scientists, they lived in conditions that were as close to natural as possible. The troop had to learn to forage for new types of food, avoid new types of predators, such as rattlesnakes, and get used to a very different climate. They adapted very well.

Now, more than 40 years later, the Texas Snow Monkey Sanctuary is home to several hundred Japanese macaques. Many scientists travel to the sanctuary to study the macaques every year. The sanctuary also provides a home for unwanted macaques from zoos and labs.

Japanese macaques are fascinating animals that need our help. You can learn more about them by joining or writing to an organization such as the Texas sanctuary:

Texas Snow Monkey Sanctuary
Dept. A
P.O. Box 702
Dilley, TX 78017

No longer strangers in their new home, Japanese macaques have managed to thrive in the hot and dry Texas climate.

Activity

Debating helps people think about ideas thoughtfully and carefully. When people debate, two sides take a different viewpoint on a subject. Each side takes turns presenting arguments to support its view.

Use the Take a Stand sections found throughout this book as a starting point for debate topics. Organize your friends or classmates into two teams. One team will argue in favor of the topic, and the other will argue against. Each team should research the issue thoroughly using reliable sources of information, including books, scientific journals, and trustworthy websites. Take notes of important facts that support your side of the debate. Prepare your argument using these facts to support your opinion.

During the debate, the members of each team are given a set amount of time to make their arguments. The team arguing the For side goes first. They have five minutes to present their case. All members of the team should participate equally. Then, the team arguing the Against side presents its arguments. Each team should take notes of the main points the other team argues.

After both teams have made their arguments, they get three minutes to prepare their rebuttals. Teams review their notes from the previous round. The teams focus on trying to disprove each of the main points made by the other team using solid facts. Each team gets three minutes to make its rebuttal. The team arguing the Against side goes first. Students and teachers watching the debate serve as judges. They should try to judge the debate fairly using a standard score sheet, such as the example below.

Criteria	Rate: 1-10	Sample Comments
1. Were the arguments well organized?	8	logical arguments, easy to follow
2. Did team members participate equally?	9	divided time evenly between members
3. Did team members speak loudly and clearly?	3	some members were difficult to hear
4. Were rebuttals specific to the other team's arguments?	6	rebuttals were specific, more facts needed
5. Was respect shown for the other team?	10	all members showed respect to the other team

Quiz

1. To which order of animals does the Japanese macaque belong?

2. What color is a macaque's face during mating season?

3. What is a macaque's most important sense?

4. True or False: Macaques live in social groups called tribes.

6. What is the Japanese macaque's biggest competitor?

5. How do Japanese macaques communicate?

7. What is the biggest threat to Japanese macaques?

8. Which part of a Japanese macaque's body can be used to temporarily store food?

9. How much does an average adult male Japanese macaque weigh?

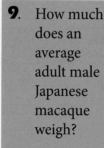

10. How often do female macaques give birth?

Answers:
1. primates 2. deep red 3. sight 4. False. Japanese macaques live in groups called troops. 5. using vocalizations, displays, and body language 6. humans 7. habitat loss 8. cheek pouch 9. 32 pounds (15 kg) 10. every 1.5 to 3 years

Key Words

adaptable: able to change to fit different conditions

ecosystems: communities of living things and resources

endangered: in danger of becoming extinct, or no longer surviving in the world

feral: a usually domestic animal, such as a dog or cat, that lives in nature and cares for itself

food web: connecting food chains that show how energy flows from one organism to another through diet

gestation period: the length of time that a female is pregnant

habitats: places where animals live, grow, and raise their young

home range: the entire area in which an animal lives

hormones: chemicals made by certain glands in the body

juvenile: a young adult

nurse: when a mammal provides its young with mother's milk

nutrition: the process of taking in food for energy

opposable: the ability to place either the first finger and thumb or the big and second toes together to grasp things

order: one of eight major ranks used to classify animals, between class and family

organisms: forms of life

primate: a large category of animals that includes prosimians, monkeys, apes, and humans

primatology: the study of primates

species: groups of individuals with common characteristics

threatened: at risk of becoming endangered

vocalizations: sounds made by animals

weaned: when a young animal does not drink milk from its mother anymore

yearlings: animals that are one year old

Index

Log on to www.av2books.com

AV² by Weigl brings you media enhanced books that support active learning. Go to www.av2books.com, and enter the special code found on page 2 of this book. You will gain access to enriched and enhanced content that supplements and complements this book. Content includes video, audio, weblinks, quizzes, a slide show, and activities.

AV² Online Navigation

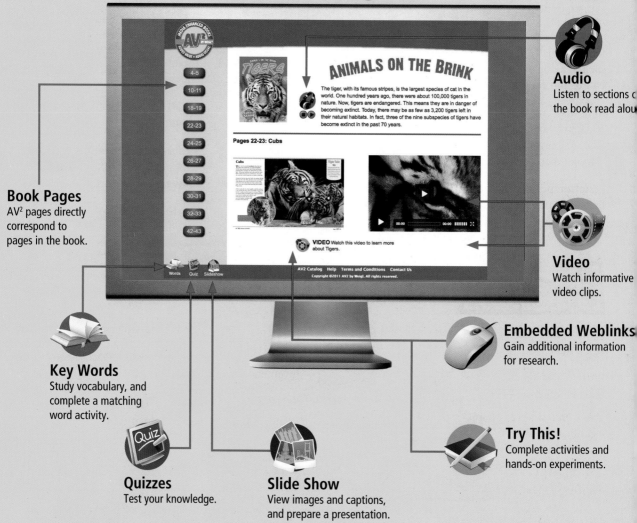

Audio
Listen to sections of the book read aloud

Book Pages
AV² pages directly correspond to pages in the book.

Video
Watch informative video clips.

Key Words
Study vocabulary, and complete a matching word activity.

Embedded Weblinks
Gain additional information for research.

Quizzes
Test your knowledge.

Slide Show
View images and captions, and prepare a presentation.

Try This!
Complete activities and hands-on experiments.

AV² was built to bridge the gap between print and digital. We encourage you to tell us what you like and what you want to see in the future.

Sign up to be an AV² Ambassador at www.av2books.com/ambassador.